The Wealth Blueprint: A Comprehensive Guide for Aspiring Entrepreneurs

AJETUNMOBI, MUKADAM OLAITAN (ALABI)

Table Of Contents

01

Chapter 1:
Understanding the
Mindset of Wealth

The Power of Belief: Shifting Your Mindset for Financial Success

In this subchapter, we delve into the transformative power of belief and how it can be harnessed to pave the way for financial success. Whether you are an aspiring entrepreneur, a career professional, a student, or simply someone seeking personal growth and financial well-being, understanding and shifting your mindset is the first step towards achieving your goals.

We begin by exploring the concept of belief and its impact on our thoughts, actions, and ultimately, our financial outcomes. Belief, as we will discover, is not just a mere thought or idea; it is a powerful force that shapes our reality. By examining our existing beliefs about money, success, and wealth, we can uncover any limiting beliefs that may be holding us back from achieving the financial success we desire.

The subchapter then delves into various strategies and techniques for shifting our mindset towards a more empowering belief system. We explore the power of affirmations, visualization, and positive self-talk in reprogramming our subconscious mind for success. Additionally, we discuss the importance of surrounding ourselves with like-minded individuals and mentors who can support and inspire us on our journey.

Through real-life examples and case studies, we illustrate how individuals from diverse backgrounds have transformed their financial situations by adopting a new belief system. From small business owners who have scaled their enterprises to investors who have made informed decisions to grow their wealth, the stories shared in this subchapter provide inspiration and practical insights for readers from all walks of life.

Finally, we emphasize the importance of taking consistent action in alignment with our new beliefs. We discuss the role of goal setting, planning, and perseverance in manifesting our financial aspirations. By combining a powerful belief system with strategic action steps, readers can unlock their full potential and create the financial success they desire.

Overall, this subchapter serves as a guide for individuals looking to shift their mindset and harness the power of belief to achieve financial success. Whether you are an aspiring entrepreneur, a career professional, a student, or someone seeking personal growth, the principles shared in this subchapter can be applied to your unique circumstances, allowing you to create a solid financial foundation and achieve greater levels of prosperity and fulfillment.

Overcoming Limiting Beliefs: Identifying and Challenging Negative Thoughts

In the pursuit of financial success, one of the biggest obstacles that individuals often face is their own limiting beliefs. These negative thoughts can hold us back, preventing us from taking risks, seizing opportunities, and achieving our full potential. However, by identifying and challenging these beliefs, we can break free from their grip and pave the way for greater financial success.

In this subchapter, we will explore the power of our thoughts and how they can either propel us forward or hold us back. We will delve into the common limiting beliefs that many individuals face, such as "I'm not smart enough," "I don't have enough money to start a business," or "Success is only for the lucky few." By recognizing these beliefs, we can begin to dissect their origins and challenge their validity.

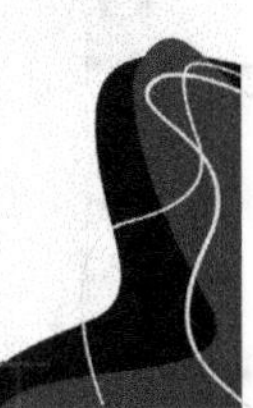

Through practical exercises and insightful anecdotes, this subchapter will guide you through the process of identifying your own limiting beliefs and reframing them into empowering thoughts. You will learn techniques to shift your mindset from one of scarcity to abundance, from self-doubt to self-confidence, and from fear to courage.

Moreover, we will explore the importance of surrounding ourselves with positive influences and supportive communities. By seeking out mentors, joining mastermind groups, and connecting with like-minded individuals, we can create an environment that fosters growth and empowers us to overcome our limiting beliefs.

The subchapter will also delve into the concept of affirmations and visualization techniques, which can be powerful tools for reprogramming our subconscious mind. By consistently repeating positive affirmations and vividly visualizing our goals, we can rewire our brains to believe in our own potential and attract the financial success we desire.

Ultimately, this subchapter aims to equip aspiring entrepreneurs, career professionals, students, and individuals seeking personal growth with the tools and mindset necessary to overcome their limiting beliefs and achieve greater financial success. By identifying and challenging negative thoughts, we can unleash our full potential, create abundance, and build a solid foundation for wealth and personal fulfillment.

Remember, becoming rich is not something that happens overnight or by doing just one thing. It requires a holistic approach that encompasses personal growth, mindset shifts, and taking consistent action towards our goals. By embarking on this journey of overcoming limiting beliefs, you are setting yourself up for a future of financial success and personal fulfillment.

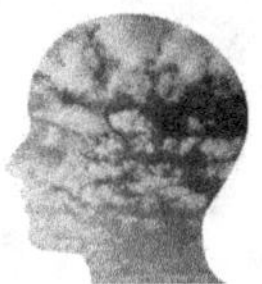

Ultimately, this subchapter aims to equip aspiring entrepreneurs, career professionals, students, and individuals seeking personal growth with the tools and mindset necessary to overcome their limiting beliefs and achieve greater financial success. By identifying and challenging negative thoughts, we can unleash our full potential, create abundance, and build a solid foundation for wealth and personal fulfillment.

Remember, becoming rich is not something that happens overnight or by doing just one thing. It requires a holistic approach that encompasses personal growth, mindset shifts, and taking consistent action towards our goals. By embarking on this journey of overcoming limiting beliefs, you are setting yourself up for a future of financial success and personal fulfillment.

In the subchapter "Cultivating an Abundance Mindset: Embracing a Positive and Wealth-Attracting Attitude," readers will discover the transformative power of adopting a mindset focused on abundance and positivity. This section of the book aims to guide aspiring entrepreneurs, career professionals, students, and individuals seeking personal growth on their journey towards financial success.

Cultivating an Abundance Mindset: Embracing a Positive and Wealth-Attracting Attitude

In the subchapter "Cultivating an Abundance Mindset: Embracing a Positive and Wealth-Attracting Attitude," readers will discover the transformative power of adopting a mindset focused on abundance and positivity. This section of the book aims to guide aspiring entrepreneurs, career professionals, students, and individuals seeking personal growth on their journey towards financial success.

The chapter begins by debunking the myth that becoming rich is an insurmountable task. It highlights the importance of shifting one's perspective from scarcity to abundance and embracing the belief that opportunities for wealth creation are abundant and within reach. By adopting this mindset, readers can unleash their full potential and open themselves up to the possibilities that lie ahead.

Throughout this subchapter, readers will learn practical strategies for cultivating an abundance mindset. From practicing gratitude and positive affirmations to visualizing success and surrounding oneself with like-minded individuals, each approach is designed to rewire the mind for success and attract wealth.

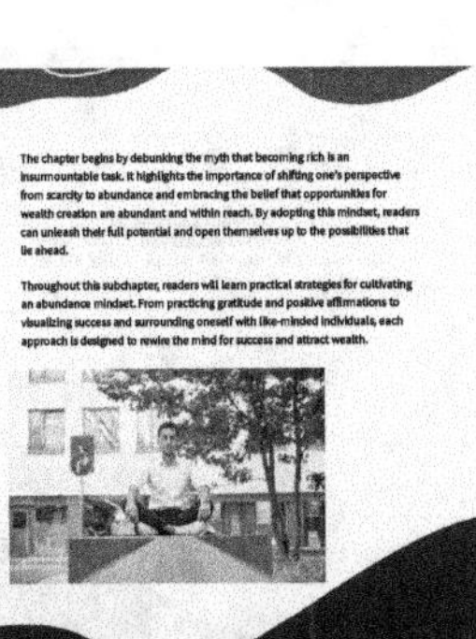

The chapter also delves into the power of self-belief and overcoming limiting beliefs that hinder financial growth. By identifying and challenging these beliefs, readers can develop the confidence to take calculated risks and seize opportunities that align with their goals.

Furthermore, the subchapter explores the concept of wealth attraction through the law of attraction. It highlights the importance of aligning one's thoughts, feelings, and actions with the desired financial outcomes. Through the law of attraction, readers will discover how their thoughts and energy can shape their reality and attract abundance into their lives.

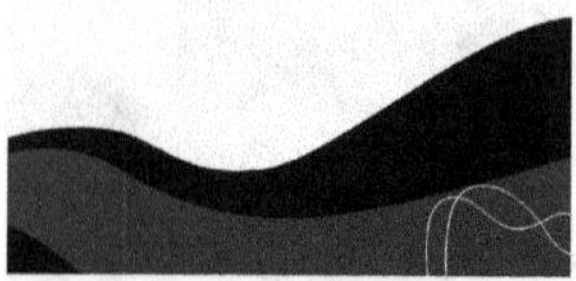

In addition to mindset shifts, readers will find practical exercises and actionable steps to incorporate into their daily lives. These activities aim to reinforce the abundance mindset and foster a positive relationship with money and wealth.

By the end of this subchapter, readers will have gained a deeper understanding of the significance of cultivating an abundance mindset and embracing a positive and wealth-attracting attitude. They will be equipped with the tools and strategies necessary to overcome limiting beliefs, tap into their full potential, and attract financial success.

entrepreneur looking to start your own business, a career professional seeking to enhance your financial well-being, or an individual seeking personal growth and financial empowerment, this subchapter will provide invaluable insights to help you achieve your goals.

The Law of Attraction: Harnessing the Power of Manifestation in Wealth Creation

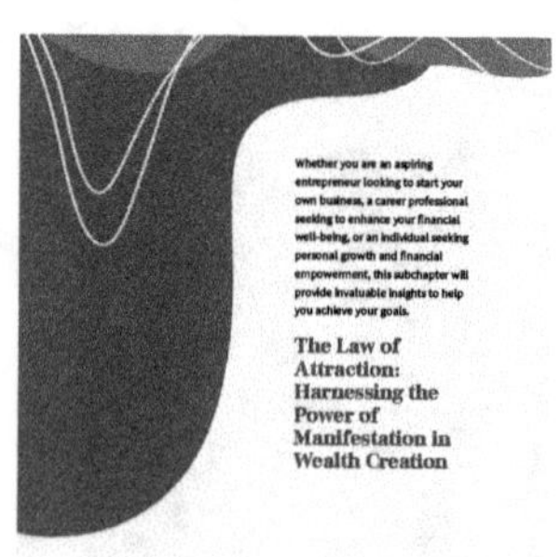

Whether you are an aspiring entrepreneur looking to start your own business, a career professional seeking to enhance your financial well-being, or an individual seeking personal growth and financial empowerment, this subchapter will provide invaluable insights to help you achieve your goals.

The Law of Attraction: Harnessing the Power of Manifestation in Wealth Creation

In the subchapter titled "The Law of Attraction: Harnessing the Power of Manifestation in Wealth Creation," we delve into a fundamental principle that can transform your financial journey and pave the way for abundant success. Whether you are an aspiring entrepreneur, a career professional, a student, or simply someone seeking personal growth and financial empowerment, understanding and applying the Law of Attraction can be a game-changer.

The Law of Attraction states that like attracts like, meaning that the thoughts and beliefs we hold in our minds have the power to attract corresponding circumstances, opportunities, and wealth into our lives. In essence, our thoughts and emotions act as magnets, pulling in the experiences and outcomes that align with our dominant mindset.

To harness the power of manifestation in wealth creation, we must first cultivate a positive and abundant mindset. This involves shifting our focus from scarcity and lack to abundance and prosperity. By consistently affirming positive beliefs about money and wealth, visualizing our desired financial outcomes, and adopting an attitude of gratitude for the abundance already present in our lives, we begin to align ourselves with the flow of wealth.

However, it is important to note that the Law of Attraction is not a magical formula that guarantees instant riches. It is a tool that, when combined with strategic action and a strong work ethic, can propel us towards our financial goals. By setting clear intentions, creating a detailed plan of action, and taking consistent steps towards our desired outcomes, we actively participate in the manifestation process.

In this subchapter, we explore practical techniques and exercises to help you harness the power of the Law of Attraction in your wealth creation journey. From creating vision boards and practicing daily affirmations to adopting a mindset of abundance and learning to let go of limiting beliefs, we provide you with a comprehensive guide to manifesting financial success.

Whether you are a financial beginner, a small business owner, an investor, or simply someone seeking personal growth and financial empowerment, the Law of Attraction offers invaluable insights and tools to help you attract wealth and achieve your financial goals. By understanding and harnessing this universal law, you can unlock the potential within yourself to create the financial abundance and personal fulfillment you desire.

Remember, becoming rich is not an elusive dream. By embracing the Law of Attraction and taking inspired action, you can manifest the wealth and success you deserve. Are you ready to tap into the power of manifestation and create a life of abundance? Let this subchapter be your guide on your journey to financial empowerment and personal growth.

Developing a Growth Mindset: Embracing Challenges and Continuous Learning

In the pursuit of financial success, one of the most vital qualities to cultivate is a growth mindset. A growth mindset is the belief that abilities and intelligence can be developed through dedication and hard work. This subchapter explores the power of embracing challenges and continuous learning as essential components of a growth mindset, providing valuable insights and strategies for individuals looking to achieve financial success.

For aspiring entrepreneurs, the path to building a successful business is often riddled with obstacles and uncertainties. Embracing challenges becomes crucial in navigating through the ups and downs of entrepreneurship. This subchapter offers practical advice on reframing challenges as opportunities for growth, fostering resilience, and maintaining a positive mindset in the face of adversity. Additionally, it emphasizes the importance of continuous learning, encouraging aspiring entrepreneurs to seek new knowledge and skills that can propel them towards success.

Career professionals seeking to enhance their financial well-being and advance their careers can also benefit from embracing challenges and continuous learning. By adopting a growth mindset, individuals can overcome self-limiting beliefs, take on new challenges, and continuously develop their skills and expertise. This subchapter provides guidance on setting ambitious goals, embracing discomfort, and seeking out learning opportunities to propel career growth and financial success.

Students and young adults, eager to establish a solid financial foundation and build wealth from an early age, can find valuable insights in this subchapter. It encourages them to embrace challenges as learning opportunities, develop a thirst for knowledge, and cultivate a growth mindset that will serve as a solid foundation for future success. By adopting a growth mindset, they can overcome obstacles, develop financial literacy, and make informed decisions that will set them on a path towards financial independence.

Furthermore, this subchapter is relevant to individuals seeking personal growth and self-improvement. It explores the interconnectedness of personal development and financial success, emphasizing that a growth mindset is not limited to wealth-building but is a powerful tool for overall personal growth. By embracing challenges and continuously learning, individuals can unlock their full potential, achieve greater financial success, and experience profound personal fulfillment.

In conclusion, this subchapter on developing a growth mindset embracing challenges and continuous learning offers valuable insights and strategies for a diverse range of readers. Whether you are an aspiring entrepreneur, career professional, student, or someone seeking personal growth and financial empowerment, the principles shared in this subchapter will guide you towards embracing challenges, cultivating a growth mindset, and achieving greater financial success.

02

Chapter 2: Building
a Strong Financial
Foundation

Setting Clear Financial Goals: Defining Your Vision for Financial Success

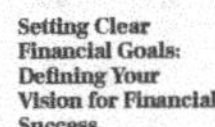

In the pursuit of financial success, one of the most vital steps is setting clear financial goals. Without a vision of where you want to be, it becomes challenging to formulate a plan to get there. This subchapter delves into the importance of defining your vision for financial success and provides practical guidance for individuals across various backgrounds and aspirations.

For aspiring entrepreneurs, this subchapter offers insights on aligning your financial goals with your business aspirations. It explores how setting clear objectives can help you establish a solid foundation for your venture and make informed decisions that contribute to its growth and success.

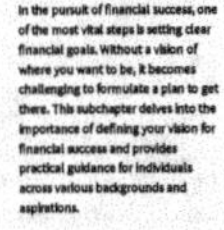

Career professionals will find value in understanding how defining financial goals can enhance their financial well-being and advance their careers. Whether it's achieving a certain income level, securing a promotion, or building a nest egg for retirement, this subchapter provides actionable strategies to set and achieve these goals.

Students and young adults can benefit from establishing a solid financial foundation early on. By defining their vision for financial success, they can learn the principles of wealth-building and make informed decisions that set them on a path towards long-term financial security.

Individuals seeking personal growth will find guidance on how setting clear financial goals can be a powerful tool for self-improvement. By aligning their financial aspirations with their personal development journey, they can achieve greater financial success while also enhancing their mindset and overall well-being.

For financial beginners, this subchapter serves as a comprehensive guide to get started on their wealth-building journey. It provides step-by-step instructions on how to define their financial goals and create a roadmap to achieve them.

Small business owners can maximize their financial potential by setting clear goals for their enterprises. This subchapter offers insights on how to align their financial aspirations with their business objectives, enabling them to grow their ventures and achieve their desired level of success.

Investors will gain valuable knowledge on investment strategies and how to make informed choices to grow their wealth. This subchapter provides a foundation for understanding the world of investments and helps individuals define their financial goals in this specific domain.

Social educators and mentors will find insights on guiding others toward financial empowerment. By understanding the process of setting clear financial goals, they can provide effective guidance and support to help others achieve their desired level of financial success.

For self-help enthusiasts, this subchapter bridges the gap between personal development and financial success. It offers practical tools and techniques for applying principles of self-improvement to enhance one's financial well-being.

Finally, for individuals seeking a holistic approach to financial success, this subchapter emphasizes the interconnectedness of personal growth, wealth-building, and higher levels of consciousness. It encourages readers to define their financial goals in alignment with their broader vision of prosperity and fulfillment.

In conclusion, this subchapter on setting clear financial goals is a valuable resource for a diverse audience seeking guidance on achieving financial success. By defining your vision for financial success, you can pave the way for a prosperous future and unlock your full potential in both personal and financial realms.

Creating a Budget: Managing Your Income and Expenses Effectively

One of the foundational steps towards achieving financial success is creating a budget that allows you to effectively manage your income and expenses. Whether you are an aspiring entrepreneur, a career professional, a student, or simply someone seeking personal growth, understanding the principles of budgeting is essential for building wealth and achieving your financial goals.

In this subchapter, we will explore the importance of creating a budget and provide practical guidance on how to do so effectively. By following these principles, you will gain control over your finances, make informed financial decisions, and pave the way for long-term financial success.

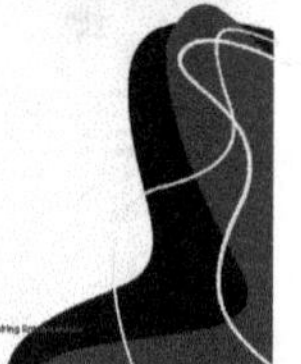

Firstly, we will delve into the significance of understanding your income. This includes not only your primary source of income but also any additional income streams you may have. By accurately assessing your income, you can determine the amount of money you have available to allocate towards different expenses and financial goals.

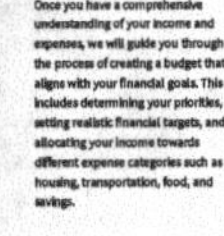

Next, we will discuss the importance of tracking your expenses. This involves keeping a record of all your expenditures, both big and small. By doing so, you will gain a clear understanding of where your money is going and identify any areas where you can cut back or make adjustments.

Once you have a comprehensive understanding of your income and expenses, we will guide you through the process of creating a budget that aligns with your financial goals. This includes determining your priorities, setting realistic financial targets, and allocating your income towards different expense categories such as housing, transportation, food, and savings.

Furthermore, we will explore strategies for effectively managing your budget on a day-to-day basis. This includes tips for reducing expenses, finding ways to increase your income, and maintaining discipline and consistency in your financial habits.

Lastly, we will address the importance of regularly reviewing and adjusting your budget. As your financial situation and goals change over time, it is crucial to revisit your budget and make necessary adjustments to ensure it remains aligned with your aspirations.

By following the principles and strategies outlined in this subchapter, you will be equipped with the tools and knowledge to create a budget that effectively manages your income and expenses. This will not only enhance your financial well-being but also contribute to your personal growth and overall success. Remember, creating a budget is not a one-time task but an ongoing process that requires dedication and discipline. Through consistent budgeting, you will be on the path towards achieving your financial goals and building long-lasting wealth.

Debt Management: Strategies for Paying Off Debt and Becoming Financially Free

In the pursuit of financial success, one crucial aspect that cannot be overlooked is debt management. Whether you are an aspiring entrepreneur, a career professional, a student, or someone seeking personal growth, understanding how to effectively manage your debts is paramount to achieving your financial goals.

In this subchapter, we will delve into strategies for paying off debt and becoming financially free, providing you with practical guidance and actionable steps to take control of your financial situation. We will explore various debt management techniques, including debt consolidation, budgeting, and negotiating with creditors, to help you create a solid plan for eliminating your debts.

For aspiring entrepreneurs, managing debt is especially critical as it can impact your ability to secure funding for your business ventures. We will discuss the importance of debt-to-income ratio and credit scores, and how they can affect your borrowing capacity. By implementing effective debt management strategies, you can position yourself for success in entrepreneurship and ensure that your business growth is not hindered by excessive debt.

Career professionals will also benefit from learning how to pay off debts and manage their finances effectively. By reducing debt burdens, you can enhance your financial well-being and create opportunities for career advancement. We will explore the concept of debt-to-income ratio and how it can impact your financial stability and decision-making. Additionally, we will provide insights on how to make informed financial choices that align with your career goals and aspirations.

Students and young adults seeking to establish a solid financial foundation will find valuable guidance in this subchapter. We will emphasize the importance of starting early and building good financial habits from a young age. From creating a realistic budget to understanding the implications of student loans, we will equip you with the knowledge and tools to make informed financial decisions that pave the way for long-term success.

Small business owners and investors can also benefit from mastering debt management strategies. By understanding how to effectively pay off debts and minimize interest payments, entrepreneurs can maximize their profits and grow their enterprises. Investors, on the other hand, will gain insights into making informed choices when it comes to leveraging debt for investment purposes and managing financial risks.

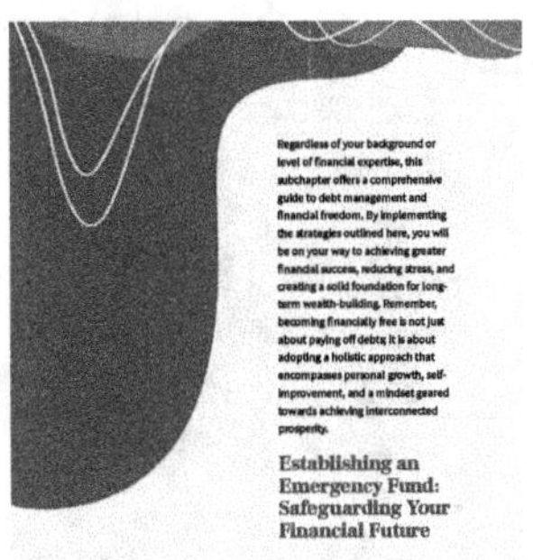

Regardless of your background or level of financial expertise, this subchapter offers a comprehensive guide to debt management and financial freedom. By implementing the strategies outlined here, you will be on your way to achieving greater financial success, reducing stress, and creating a solid foundation for long-term wealth-building. Remember, becoming financially free is not just about paying off debts; it is about adopting a holistic approach that encompasses personal growth, self-improvement, and a mindset geared towards achieving interconnected prosperity.

Establishing an Emergency Fund: Safeguarding Your Financial Future

In this subchapter, "Establishing an Emergency Fund: Safeguarding Your Financial Future," we will delve into the importance of having an emergency fund and how it can protect your financial well-being. Whether you are an aspiring entrepreneur, a career professional, a student, or anyone seeking financial success, this chapter will provide valuable insights on building a solid financial foundation.

An emergency fund is a crucial component of any comprehensive financial plan. It acts as a safety net during unexpected circumstances such as job loss, medical emergencies, or unforeseen expenses. Without an emergency fund, individuals may find themselves relying on credit cards, loans, or depleting their savings, which can lead to financial instability and stress.

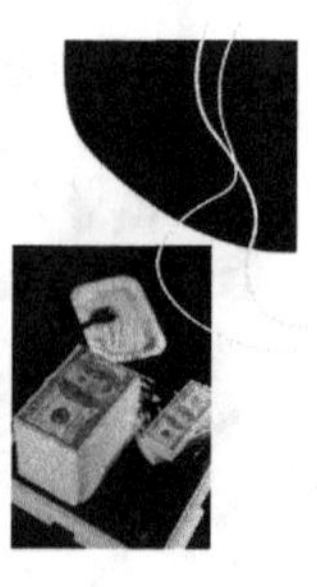

For aspiring entrepreneurs, having an emergency fund is vital as it provides a buffer during the initial stages of starting a business. It allows you to have peace of mind knowing that you can cover essential expenses and unforeseen setbacks without compromising your venture's success.

Career professionals can also benefit from establishing an emergency fund. It ensures that they have a financial cushion in case of sudden job loss or unexpected expenses. With an emergency fund in place, individuals can focus on their career growth and make informed financial decisions without worrying about immediate financial obligations.

Students and young adults who establish an emergency fund early on set themselves up for a solid financial future. By developing the habit of saving and being prepared for unexpected events, they gain a sense of financial security and independence.

Small business owners and investors can leverage an emergency fund to protect their enterprises and investments. It provides a safety net during economic downturns, market fluctuations, or unexpected business expenses. With an emergency fund, entrepreneurs can weather challenging times and avoid making rash financial decisions that could jeopardize their long-term goals.

In this subchapter, we will discuss practical strategies to build and maintain an emergency fund. We will explore the ideal amount to save, how to prioritize savings, and where to allocate the funds for maximum security and growth. Additionally, we will address common misconceptions about emergency funds and offer tips to overcome challenges in establishing and sustaining this essential financial resource.

By establishing an emergency fund, you are taking a proactive step towards safeguarding your financial future. It provides a sense of security, peace of mind, and the ability to navigate unexpected events without derailing your financial goals. Whether you are an aspiring entrepreneur, a career professional, a student, or someone seeking personal growth, this subchapter will equip you with the knowledge and tools to establish and maintain an emergency fund that will protect your financial well-being and pave the way for long-term success.

Saving and Investing: Growing Your Wealth through Strategic Financial Planning

In this subchapter, we will explore the essential concepts of saving and investing, and how they can help you grow your wealth through strategic financial planning. Whether you are an aspiring entrepreneur, a career professional, a student, or simply someone seeking personal growth and financial empowerment, understanding these principles is crucial for achieving long-term financial success.

Saving and investing are two fundamental pillars of wealth-building. Saving involves setting aside a portion of your income for future use, while investing refers to putting your money into various assets or ventures with the expectation of generating a return. By combining both strategies, you can create a powerful financial plan that will pave the way to financial freedom.

We will start by discussing the importance of saving and creating a budget that allows you to allocate a portion of your income towards savings. We will provide practical tips on how to reduce expenses, increase income, and develop a disciplined savings habit. Saving is the foundation upon which you can build your wealth, and it is crucial to establish a solid financial cushion to weather any unforeseen circumstances.

Once you have a robust savings plan in place, we will delve into the world of investing. We will explore different investment vehicles such as stocks, bonds, real estate, and mutual funds, and provide insights on how to make informed investment choices. We will discuss the concept of risk and return, diversification, and the importance of long-term investing.

Furthermore, we will introduce you to various investment strategies, such as dollar-cost averaging, value investing, and asset allocation. We will also emphasize the significance of seeking professional advice and conducting thorough research before making any investment decisions.

Throughout this subchapter, we will provide real-life examples, case studies, and practical exercises to help you apply the principles of saving and investing to your own financial journey. We will also address common misconceptions and myths surrounding wealth-building, debunking the notion that becoming rich is easy and requires only one magic formula.

By the end of this subchapter, you will have a comprehensive understanding of how saving and investing can help you grow your wealth strategically. You will be equipped with the knowledge and tools to make informed financial decisions, and you will be inspired to take action towards achieving your financial goals. Whether you are a beginner or an experienced investor, this subchapter will serve as a valuable resource in your pursuit of financial success and personal growth.

03
Chapter 3:
Entrepreneurship and
Business Strategies

Identifying Your Passion and Purpose: Finding the Right Business Idea

In the journey towards financial success, one of the most crucial steps is identifying your passion and purpose. This is especially important when it comes to starting your own business or venture. The right business idea is not just about making money, but also about finding fulfillment and creating something meaningful.

For aspiring entrepreneurs, it is essential to align your business idea with your passion and purpose. This means identifying what truly excites and motivates you. Take the time to explore your interests, hobbies, and skills. What are you naturally good at? What do you enjoy doing in your free time? Reflect on these questions and use them as a starting point to generate business ideas.

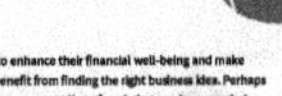

Career professionals looking to enhance their financial well-being and make informed decisions can also benefit from finding the right business idea. Perhaps you have skills or expertise in your current line of work that can be expanded upon or turned into a profitable venture. Consider how you can leverage your existing knowledge and experience to create a business that aligns with your goals.

For students and young adults, establishing a solid financial foundation is crucial. Finding the right business idea at an early age can set you on the path to long-term success. Take advantage of your youthful energy and enthusiasm to explore different industries and opportunities. Embrace a growth mindset and be open to learning from failures and setbacks. This will not only help you find the right business idea but also build resilience and determination.

Even for those new to the world of personal finance and wealth-building, finding the right business idea can be a transformative experience. This book provides a comprehensive guide to help financial beginners navigate the process of identifying their passion and purpose. It offers practical tips, exercises, and insights to help you discover your unique strengths and interests.

Small business owners and investors can also benefit from reevaluating their current ventures and exploring new business ideas. As the business landscape evolves, it is crucial to stay ahead of the curve and adapt to changing market demands. This subchapter provides strategies for identifying new opportunities and maximizing financial potential.

Regardless of your background or current situation, finding the right business idea is a crucial step towards financial success. This subchapter offers practical guidance and exercises to help you identify your passion and purpose. It encourages you to think outside the box, embrace personal growth, and pursue a business idea that aligns with your goals and values. By taking the time to identify your passion and purpose, you can create a business that not only generates wealth but also brings you joy and fulfilment.

Market Research and Analysis: Understanding Your Target Audience and Competition

In today's competitive business landscape, understanding your target audience and competition is crucial for achieving financial success. Whether you're an aspiring entrepreneur, a career professional, a student, or simply someone seeking personal growth, conducting market research and analysis is a fundamental step towards building a solid foundation for wealth-building.

For aspiring entrepreneurs, market research allows you to identify and understand your target audience's needs, preferences, and pain points. By gathering data on their demographics, psychographics, and purchasing behaviors, you can tailor your products or services to meet their specific demands. Additionally, analyzing your competitors' strategies and offerings can provide valuable insights, enabling you to differentiate yourself and gain a competitive edge.

Career professionals can also benefit from market research and analysis to enhance their financial well-being and advance their careers. By understanding the current market trends, identifying high-demand skills, and analyzing industry competition, you can make informed decisions about your professional development. This knowledge can help you position yourself as a sought-after professional, increase your earning potential, and seize lucrative opportunities.

Students and young adults can lay the groundwork for financial success by learning the principles of wealth-building at an early age. Conducting market research can teach them about the importance of identifying target audiences, understanding consumer behavior, and recognizing market gaps. Armed with this knowledge, they can make informed financial decisions, whether it's starting a side business, investing in stocks, or launching a startup.

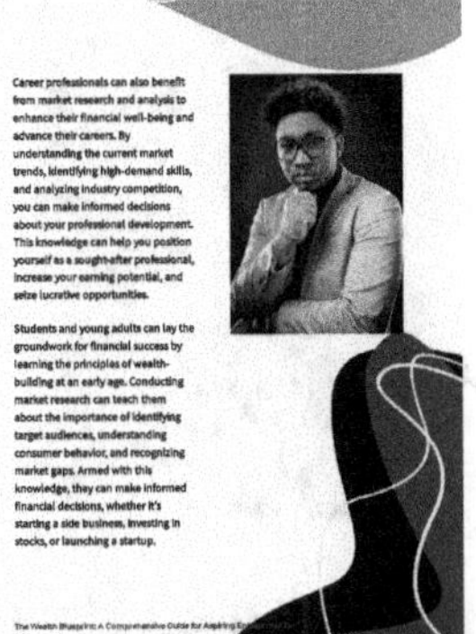

Financial beginners will find this subchapter invaluable as it provides a comprehensive guide to understanding market research and analysis. By breaking down complex concepts into easily digestible information, it demystifies the world of personal finance and wealth-building.

It equips them with the tools and knowledge needed to navigate the market, make informed investment choices, and create a solid financial plan.

Small business owners can leverage market research and analysis to grow their enterprises and maximize their financial potential. By identifying their target audience's needs and preferences, they can tailor their products or services to meet market demands. Additionally, analyzing their competitors' strategies can help them stay ahead of the curve and identify untapped opportunities.

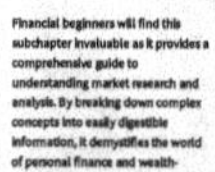

Investors looking to grow their wealth can benefit from understanding market research and analysis. By studying different investment strategies, analyzing market trends, and assessing risk factors, they can make informed choices that align with their financial goals. This subchapter provides insights into various investment avenues, such as stocks, real estate, and mutual funds, empowering investors to make well-rounded financial decisions.

Investors looking to grow their wealth can benefit from understanding market research and analysis. By studying different investment strategies, analyzing market trends, and assessing risk factors, they can make informed choices that align with their financial goals. This subchapter provides insights into various investment avenues, such as stocks, real estate, and mutual funds, empowering investors to make well-rounded financial decisions.

Social educators and mentors involved in guiding others towards financial empowerment can gain valuable insights from this subchapter. Understanding market research and analysis allows them to equip their students or mentees with the knowledge and skills needed to succeed in the business world. By incorporating these principles into their teachings, they can empower others to make informed financial decisions and achieve greater financial success.

Self-help enthusiasts will find this subchapter a valuable addition to their personal development journey. It combines the principles of self-improvement with financial success, offering a holistic approach to wealth-building. By understanding market research and analysis, they can apply these principles to their financial goals, creating a mindset of abundance and prosperity.

Lastly, individuals seeking a holistic approach to financial success will find this subchapter enlightening. It goes beyond traditional wealth-building strategies and delves into interconnected prosperity and higher levels of consciousness. By understanding market dynamics, they can align their financial pursuits with their values and contribute to a more sustainable and fulfilling world.

"The Wealth Blueprint: A Comprehensive Guide for Aspiring Entrepreneurs" caters to a diverse audience eager to enhance their financial well-being and personal growth. By providing insights into market research and analysis, it equips readers with the knowledge and tools needed to navigate the business world successfully. Whether you're an aspiring entrepreneur, a career professional, a student, or someone seeking personal development, this book is a valuable resource on the path to financial success.

Creating a Business Plan: Mapping Out Your Path to Success

In the journey of entrepreneurship, having a well-thought-out business plan is like having a roadmap that guides you towards your desired destination. Whether you are an aspiring entrepreneur, a small business owner, or a career professional looking to enhance your financial well-being, creating a business plan is essential to your success. This subchapter titled "Creating a Business Plan: Mapping Out Your Path to Success" provides a comprehensive guide on how to develop a solid business plan that aligns with your goals and maximizes your potential for financial success.

The subchapter begins by emphasizing the importance of crafting a clear vision and mission statement for your business. It highlights the significance of setting specific, measurable, attainable, relevant, and time-bound (SMART) goals that serve as milestones along your entrepreneurial journey. By outlining your objectives and understanding your target market, you can create a business plan that addresses the needs and demands of your customers, setting you apart from your competitors.

Additionally, this subchapter delves into the components of a well-rounded business plan. It provides insights into conducting market research, identifying your unique selling proposition, and conducting a competitive analysis. By understanding your industry landscape and the strengths and weaknesses of your competitors, you can position your business for success.

Furthermore, the subchapter explores the importance of financial planning within your business plan. It guides you through the process of creating a budget, projecting sales and expenses, and determining your break-even point. By having a solid financial plan in place, you can make informed decisions, secure financing, and navigate potential challenges along the way.

Moreover, this subchapter emphasizes the significance of regularly reviewing and updating your business plan. It encourages you to adapt to market trends, embrace innovation, and remain agile in an ever-changing business environment.

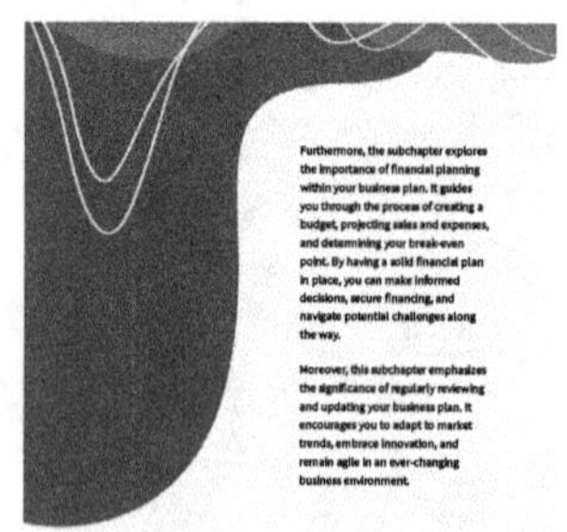

Furthermore, the subchapter explores the importance of financial planning within your business plan. It guides you through the process of creating a budget, projecting sales and expenses, and determining your break-even point. By having a solid financial plan in place, you can make informed decisions, secure financing, and navigate potential challenges along the way.

Moreover, this subchapter emphasizes the significance of regularly reviewing and updating your business plan. It encourages you to adapt to market trends, embrace innovation, and remain agile in an ever-changing business environment.

Whether you are an aspiring entrepreneur, a small business owner, or a career professional aiming to enhance your financial well-being, creating a business plan is crucial to your success. By mapping out your path to success and building a comprehensive plan, you can achieve your goals, maximize your potential, and create a solid foundation for long-term financial success.

This subchapter, "Creating a Business Plan: Mapping Out Your Path to Success," provides valuable insights, practical tips, and actionable steps to guide you through the process of creating a business plan tailored to your specific needs and aspirations. Whether you are a financial beginner, a seasoned entrepreneur, or someone seeking personal growth and development, this subchapter offers a holistic approach to achieving financial success and personal fulfillment.

Funding Your Business: Exploring Financing Options and Resources

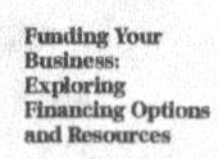

Starting a business or venture can be an exciting endeavor, but one of the most crucial aspects is securing the necessary funding. In this subchapter, we will delve into the various financing options and resources available to aspiring entrepreneurs, small business owners, and anyone seeking financial success.

For individuals looking to start their own businesses, understanding the different avenues for financing is essential. We will explore traditional options such as bank loans, lines of credit, and Small Business Administration (SBA) loans. Additionally, we will discuss alternative funding sources like crowdfunding, angel investors, and venture capital, highlighting their benefits and potential drawbacks.

Career professionals aiming to enhance their financial well-being and make informed financial decisions will find valuable insights in this subchapter. We will explore personal financing options such as personal loans, home equity loans, and retirement account loans. We will also discuss the importance of building an emergency fund and developing a solid credit history to establish a strong financial foundation.

Students and young adults seeking to establish a solid financial footing will benefit from the principles of wealth-building discussed in this subchapter. We will provide guidance on saving strategies, budgeting, and the importance of establishing good credit early on. We will also explore resources available to students, such as scholarships, grants, and student loans, and discuss the potential long-term effects of student loan debt.

Small business owners looking to grow their enterprises and maximize their financial potential will find this subchapter invaluable. We will delve into strategies for securing funding for business expansion, including options like business credit cards, equipment financing, and invoice factoring. We will also discuss the importance of financial planning, cash flow management, and leveraging technology to optimize business operations.

Investors will gain insights into investment strategies and making informed choices to grow their wealth. We will explore different investment vehicles such as stocks, bonds, mutual funds, real estate, and alternative investments. We will discuss risk management, diversification, and the importance of understanding one's risk tolerance and investment goals.

Social educators and mentors involved in guiding others toward financial empowerment will find valuable lessons in this subchapter. We will discuss financial literacy programs, mentorship opportunities, and resources available to help individuals develop a solid understanding of personal finance and wealth-building.

Finally, this subchapter will appeal to self-help enthusiasts seeking a holistic approach to financial success. We will explore principles of personal development, self-improvement, and enhancing one's mindset to achieve greater financial success. We will discuss the interconnectedness of personal growth and financial well-being and how a holistic approach can lead to higher levels of consciousness and prosperity.

"The Wealth Blueprint: A Comprehensive Guide for Aspiring Entrepreneurs" offers a comprehensive and multifaceted approach to achieving financial success. Whether you are an aspiring entrepreneur, a seasoned professional, a student, or an individual seeking personal growth, this book provides valuable insights and resources to help you navigate the world of financing and wealth-building.

Marketing and Sales Strategies: Promoting Your Business and Generating Revenue

Marketing and sales strategies are essential for promoting your business and generating revenue. In this subchapter, we will explore various tactics and techniques that aspiring entrepreneurs can utilize to achieve financial success. Whether you are just starting your own business or looking to grow your existing enterprise, understanding effective marketing and sales strategies is crucial.

For aspiring entrepreneurs, marketing is the key to gaining visibility and attracting customers. We will discuss the importance of market research to identify your target audience and understand their needs and preferences. By conducting thorough research, you can develop a unique selling proposition that sets your business apart from competitors. We will also delve into the various channels and platforms available for promoting your business, such as social media, content marketing, and influencer partnerships.

In addition to marketing, we will explore the art of selling. Sales strategies are vital for closing deals and generating revenue. We will discuss the importance of building relationships with potential clients and developing effective sales techniques, such as active listening, objection handling, and creating a sense of urgency. Understanding the psychology of sales and mastering the art of persuasion will be key topics in this subchapter.

Furthermore, we will delve into the world of online marketing and sales. As technology continues to advance, it is crucial for entrepreneurs to leverage digital platforms to reach a wider audience. We will discuss the fundamentals of search engine optimization (SEO), pay-per-click (PPC) advertising, email marketing, and conversion rate optimization (CRO). These strategies will help you optimize your online presence and drive traffic to your website or online store.

Lastly, we will explore the importance of tracking and analyzing your marketing and sales efforts. By utilizing analytics tools and metrics, you can measure the effectiveness of your strategies and make data-driven decisions. We will discuss key performance indicators (KPIs) and how to use them to optimize your marketing and sales campaigns.

In conclusion, marketing and sales strategies are essential for promoting your business and generating revenue. This subchapter will provide aspiring entrepreneurs with valuable insights and practical tips to enhance their marketing and sales efforts. By implementing these strategies, you can effectively promote your business, attract customers, and achieve financial success.

04

Chapter 4: Leveraging Technology and Digital Platforms

Digital Marketing: Harnessing the Power of Online Advertising and Social Media

In today's digital age, harnessing the power of online advertising and social media is essential for any aspiring entrepreneur or small business owner looking to achieve financial success. The world has become increasingly interconnected through the internet, and this subchapter of "The Wealth Blueprint: A Comprehensive Guide for Aspiring Entrepreneurs" delves into the strategies and techniques of digital marketing that can propel your business to new heights.

For aspiring entrepreneurs, digital marketing offers a cost-effective way to reach a wider audience and build brand awareness. By leveraging online advertising platforms such as Google Ads and Facebook Ads, entrepreneurs can target their ideal customers and generate leads. This subchapter explores the fundamentals of online advertising, including keyword research, ad copywriting, and campaign optimization, to help you make the most of your advertising budget.

Social media has revolutionized the way businesses connect with their customers. Platforms like Facebook, Instagram, and LinkedIn provide opportunities for entrepreneurs to engage with their target audience, build a loyal following, and drive traffic to their websites or online stores. This subchapter delves into social media marketing strategies, including content creation, community management, and influencer collaborations, to help you effectively utilize these platforms for business growth.

Not only is digital marketing crucial for entrepreneurs, but it is also beneficial for career professionals looking to enhance their financial well-being and advance their careers. By developing a strong personal brand online and showcasing your expertise through content marketing, you can position yourself as a thought leader in your industry. This subchapter explores the various avenues of content marketing, including blogging, podcasting, and video production, to help you establish your online presence and attract new opportunities.

Furthermore, students and young adults can benefit greatly from understanding the principles of digital marketing. By learning these skills early on, they can establish a solid foundation for their future careers or entrepreneurial endeavors. This subchapter provides practical tips and guidance for young individuals to navigate the digital landscape and leverage online advertising and social media to their advantage.

In conclusion, digital marketing is a powerful tool that can help individuals from various backgrounds achieve financial success. Whether you are an aspiring entrepreneur, a career professional, a student, or simply someone seeking personal growth and financial empowerment, this subchapter of "The Wealth Blueprint" will equip you with the knowledge and strategies to harness the power of online advertising and social media. By embracing these digital marketing techniques, you can take your business, career, or personal brand to new heights and pave the way for financial prosperity.

E-Commerce and Online Marketplaces: Expanding Your Reach and Sales Channels

In today's digital age, the world of business and commerce has undergone a significant transformation. The rise of e-commerce and online marketplaces has revolutionized the way we buy and sell products and services.

For aspiring entrepreneurs, career professionals, students, and individuals seeking personal growth, harnessing the power of e-commerce can be a game-changer in achieving financial success.

This subchapter, titled "E-Commerce and Online Marketplaces: Expanding Your Reach and Sales Channels," provides valuable insights and practical guidance on how to leverage the opportunities presented by the digital marketplace. Whether you are a small business owner looking to grow your enterprise or an individual seeking to establish a solid financial foundation, this subchapter will equip you with the knowledge and strategies to maximize your reach and sales potential.

The first section of this subchapter delves into the fundamentals of e-commerce, explaining the various types of online marketplaces and the benefits they offer. It explores the advantages of selling products or services online, such as reaching a global audience, reducing overhead costs, and accessing valuable customer data. Readers will gain a comprehensive understanding of the e-commerce landscape and how it can be harnessed to their advantage.

The subsequent sections of this subchapter provide practical tips and strategies for establishing and optimizing an online presence. From creating a user-friendly website and implementing effective marketing strategies to utilizing social media platforms and optimizing search engine rankings, readers will learn how to build a strong online presence that resonates with their target audience.

The first section of this subchapter delves into the fundamentals of e-commerce, explaining the various types of online marketplaces and the benefits they offer. It explores the advantages of selling products or services online, such as reaching a global audience, reducing overhead costs, and accessing valuable customer data. Readers will gain a comprehensive understanding of the e-commerce landscape and how it can be harnessed to their advantage.

The subsequent sections of this subchapter provide practical tips and strategies for establishing and optimizing an online presence. From creating a user-friendly website and implementing effective marketing strategies to utilizing social media platforms and optimizing search engine rankings, readers will learn how to build a strong online presence that resonates with their target audience.

Furthermore, this subchapter delves into the intricacies of online marketplaces, such as Amazon, eBay, and Shopify. It provides step-by-step guidance on how to set up a seller account, navigate the platform's features, and optimize product listings for maximum visibility and sales. Readers will also gain insights into effective pricing strategies, customer service, and managing inventory to ensure a seamless online shopping experience for their customers.

Furthermore, this subchapter delves into the intricacies of online marketplaces, such as Amazon, eBay, and Shopify. It provides step-by-step guidance on how to set up a seller account, navigate the platform's features, and optimize product listings for maximum visibility and sales. Readers will also gain insights into effective pricing strategies, customer service, and managing inventory to ensure a seamless online shopping experience for their customers.

By embracing e-commerce and online marketplaces, aspiring entrepreneurs, career professionals, students, and individuals seeking personal growth can expand their reach, tap into new sales channels, and unlock their full financial potential. This subchapter serves as a comprehensive guide, offering insights and strategies tailored to the diverse needs and goals of its readers. Whether you are new to the world of e-commerce or seeking to enhance your existing online presence, this subchapter will empower you to thrive in the digital marketplace and achieve financial success.

Building a Strong Online Presence: Website Development and Search Engine Optimization

In today's digital age, having a strong online presence is crucial for individuals and businesses alike. Whether you are an aspiring entrepreneur looking to start your own business or a career professional aiming to enhance your financial well-being, building a robust online presence is a key step towards achieving success. This subchapter explores the importance of website development and search engine optimization (SEO) in creating a solid foundation for your online presence.

For aspiring entrepreneurs, a well-designed and user-friendly website serves as a virtual storefront, showcasing your products or services to potential customers. It is your online identity and the first impression that potential clients will have of your business. This subchapter provides guidance on how to develop a website that not only looks professional but also effectively communicates your brand's values and offerings.

In addition to website development, search engine optimization plays a crucial role in driving traffic to your site. SEO involves strategies and techniques that improve your website's visibility on search engine results pages. By optimizing your website for relevant keywords and ensuring that it meets search engine criteria, you can attract organic traffic and increase your chances of reaching your target audience. This subchapter delves into the various SEO tactics and best practices that can help you rank higher in search engine rankings.

Moreover, this subchapter emphasizes the importance of a holistic approach to online presence. It highlights the interconnectedness between website development, SEO, and other aspects of digital marketing, such as content creation, social media engagement, and online advertising. By understanding how all these elements work together, you can create a comprehensive online strategy that maximizes your reach and impact.

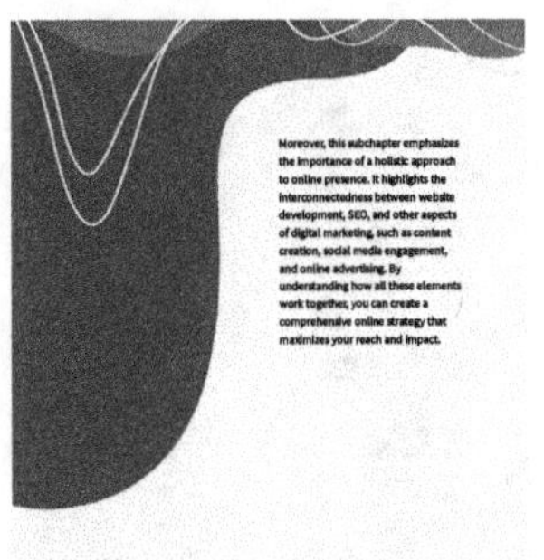

Whether you are a small business owner, a career professional, or a student seeking to establish a solid financial foundation, this subchapter provides practical insights and actionable steps to build a strong online presence. By following the strategies outlined in this chapter, you can increase your visibility, attract more customers or clients, and ultimately achieve financial success. Remember, building a strong online presence is not a one-time task but an ongoing process that requires consistent effort and adaptation to stay ahead in the ever-evolving digital landscape.

Automation and Productivity Tools: Streamlining Your Business Operations

In today's fast-paced and competitive business environment, efficiency and productivity are key factors in achieving financial success. As an aspiring entrepreneur, career professional, student, or small business owner, it is crucial to find ways to streamline your business operations and maximize your financial potential.

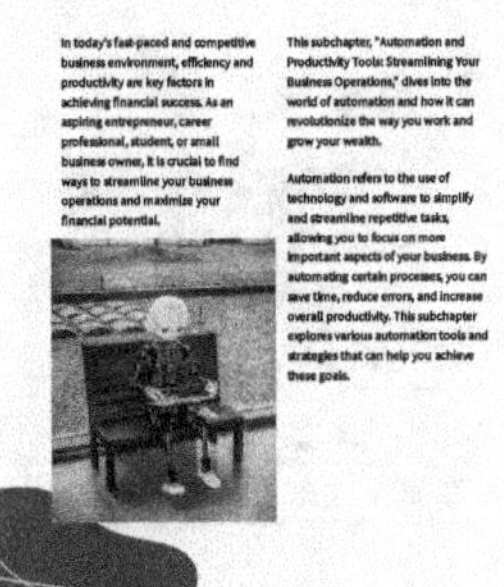

This subchapter, "Automation and Productivity Tools: Streamlining Your Business Operations," dives into the world of automation and how it can revolutionize the way you work and grow your wealth.

Automation refers to the use of technology and software to simplify and streamline repetitive tasks, allowing you to focus on more important aspects of your business. By automating certain processes, you can save time, reduce errors, and increase overall productivity. This subchapter explores various automation tools and strategies that can help you achieve these goals.

One of the key benefits of automation is its ability to free up your time and mental energy, allowing you to focus on high-value activities such as strategic planning, networking, and innovation. We discuss how automation can help you delegate repetitive tasks, such as email management, social media scheduling, and data entry, to free up valuable time for more important endeavors.

Additionally, this subchapter delves into the world of productivity tools, which go hand in hand with automation. Productivity tools are designed to enhance your efficiency and effectiveness, enabling you to accomplish more in less time. We explore a variety of productivity tools, such as project management software, task management apps, and collaboration platforms, that can streamline your workflow and boost your productivity.

Moreover, we provide practical tips and best practices on how to integrate automation and productivity tools into your daily operations. We discuss how to assess your business needs, select the right tools for your specific requirements, and implement them effectively. We also address common concerns and challenges that may arise during the automation process and provide guidance on how to overcome them.

By embracing automation and productivity tools, you can transform your business operations and propel yourself towards financial success. Whether you are a small business owner looking to scale your enterprise, a career professional aiming to enhance your productivity, or an aspiring entrepreneur seeking guidance on how to streamline your business processes, this subchapter will provide you with valuable insights and practical strategies to achieve your goals.

Remember, becoming wealthy is not an elusive dream. With the right mindset and the right tools, you can take control of your financial future and create the life of abundance you desire. The key is to embrace automation and productivity tools as powerful allies on your journey to success.

Data Analytics and Insights: Utilizing Technology to Make Informed Business Decisions

In today's digital age, data is king. It is the driving force behind successful businesses and ventures, allowing entrepreneurs to make informed decisions and maximize their financial potential. In this subchapter, we will explore the power of data analytics and how it can be harnessed to achieve financial success.

For aspiring entrepreneurs, data analytics can be a game-changer. By leveraging technology and analyzing relevant data, you can gain valuable insights into market trends, customer preferences, and industry dynamics. This knowledge allows you to make informed business decisions, identify opportunities, and stay ahead of the competition. Whether you are launching a startup or planning to expand your existing venture, data analytics can provide you with a solid foundation for success.

Career professionals can also benefit from harnessing the power of data analytics. By understanding market trends and industry demands, you can enhance your skillset and make strategic career choices. Whether it's acquiring new certifications, developing specialized expertise, or identifying emerging job opportunities, data analytics can guide you towards advancing your career and achieving financial well-being.

Students and young adults have a unique advantage when it comes to data analytics. By learning the principles of data analysis and adopting a data-driven mindset from an early age, they can establish a solid financial foundation and set themselves up for long-term success. Whether it's understanding personal finance, making informed investment choices, or starting their own businesses, data analytics can be a powerful tool for young people looking to build wealth and create a secure future.

For those seeking personal growth and self-improvement, data analytics can offer valuable insights. By analyzing your own financial data and tracking your progress, you can gain a deeper understanding of your spending habits, saving patterns, and areas for improvement. This self-awareness can empower you to make positive changes, develop healthy financial habits, and achieve greater financial success.

Small business owners and entrepreneurs can leverage data analytics to grow their enterprises and maximize their financial potential. By analyzing customer data, sales metrics, and operational efficiency, you can identify areas of improvement, optimize processes, and make data-driven decisions to drive growth and profitability. Whether it's customer segmentation, pricing strategies, or supply chain optimization, data analytics can provide you with the insights needed to take your business to the next level.

Investors can also benefit from data analytics. By analyzing market trends, economic indicators, and company data, investors can make informed choices and maximize their returns. Whether it's stock market analysis, real estate investment strategies, or portfolio diversification, data analytics can guide investors towards making sound financial decisions and growing their wealth.

Social educators and mentors can use data analytics to empower others towards financial empowerment. By understanding the power of data, educators can equip their students with the necessary skills to navigate the complex world of personal finance and make informed choices. By guiding others towards financial literacy and providing them with the tools to analyze data, mentors can empower individuals to take control of their financial well-being and achieve their goals.

For self-help enthusiasts, data analytics can be a powerful tool for personal growth and financial success. By analyzing personal data, setting goals, and tracking progress, individuals can gain insights into their own behaviors, patterns, and beliefs. This self-awareness can empower individuals to make positive changes, develop a growth mindset, and achieve their financial aspirations.

In conclusion, data analytics and insights are essential tools for individuals on the path to financial success. Whether you are an aspiring entrepreneur, a career professional, a student, or an individual seeking personal growth, data analytics can guide you towards making informed decisions and maximizing your financial potential. By harnessing the power of technology and adopting a data-driven mindset, you can create a solid foundation for success and achieve your goals.

Lastly, for those seeking a holistic approach to financial success, data analytics can be integrated with personal development principles. By combining data-driven decision-making with mindfulness, gratitude, and higher levels of consciousness, individuals can achieve interconnected prosperity. This holistic perspective recognizes that financial success is not just about wealth-building but also personal growth, fulfillment, and making a positive impact in the world.

In conclusion, data analytics and insights are essential tools for individuals on the path to financial success. Whether you are an aspiring entrepreneur, a career professional, a student, or an individual seeking personal growth, data analytics can guide you towards making informed decisions and maximizing your financial potential. By harnessing the power of technology and adopting a data-driven mindset, you can create a solid foundation for success and achieve your goals.

05
Chapter 5: Wealth Preservation and Growth Strategies
The Wealth Blueprint: A Comprehensive Guide for Aspiring Entrepreneurs
Page 74

Estate Planning: Protecting Your Assets and Ensuring Smooth Transitions

In the journey to financial success, it is crucial to not only focus on wealth accumulation but also on protecting and preserving your hard-earned assets. Estate planning plays a pivotal role in safeguarding your wealth and ensuring a smooth transition of assets to future generations. This subchapter titled "Estate Planning: Protecting Your Assets and Ensuring Smooth Transitions" delves into the importance of estate planning and provides valuable insights for aspiring entrepreneurs, career professionals, students, and anyone seeking personal growth and financial empowerment.

For aspiring entrepreneurs, estate planning is an essential component of building a successful business empire. It involves creating a comprehensive plan to protect your business assets, intellectual property, and ensuring a seamless transfer of ownership in the event of unforeseen circumstances. By addressing key aspects such as business succession, tax planning, and asset protection strategies, you can safeguard the future of your business and leave a lasting legacy.

Career professionals can greatly benefit from estate planning as well. By proactively planning for the future, you can protect your hard-earned assets and ensure financial security for your loved ones. Estate planning helps you navigate complex legal and financial matters, such as wills, trusts, and asset distribution, enabling you to make informed decisions that align with your long-term goals.

Students and young adults who aspire to achieve financial success can establish a solid foundation by understanding the principles of estate planning early on. Learning about wills, trusts, and power of attorney can provide them with a roadmap for protecting their assets and making responsible financial decisions as they embark on their professional journeys. By adopting a proactive approach to estate planning, young individuals can set themselves up for a future of financial security and stability.

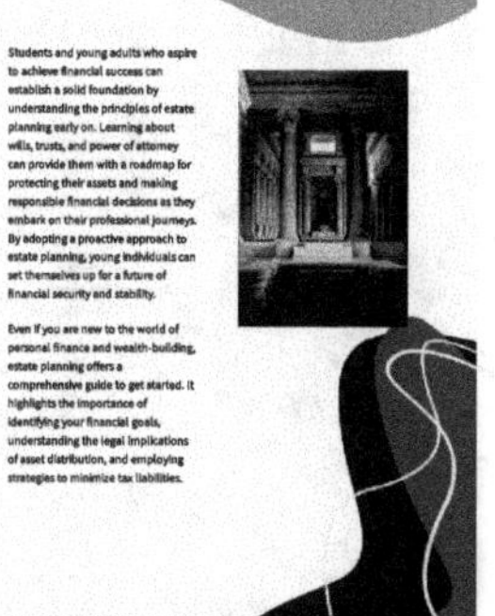

Even if you are new to the world of personal finance and wealth-building, estate planning offers a comprehensive guide to get started. It highlights the importance of identifying your financial goals, understanding the legal implications of asset distribution, and employing strategies to minimize tax liabilities.

By gaining a solid foundation in estate planning, financial beginners can take control of their financial destinies and make informed choices that align with their values and aspirations.

Small business owners, investors, social educators, mentors, self-help enthusiasts, and individuals seeking a holistic approach to financial success can all benefit from the insights provided in this subchapter. Estate planning is a vital component of a comprehensive wealth-building strategy, ensuring that your assets are protected, your loved ones are provided for, and your legacy is preserved.

In conclusion, estate planning is a critical aspect of achieving financial success and personal fulfillment. This subchapter serves as a comprehensive guide for individuals across various niches, offering valuable insights and strategies to protect your assets and ensure smooth transitions. By embracing estate planning, you can build a solid financial foundation, safeguard your wealth, and leave a lasting legacy for future generations.

Tax Planning and Strategies: Maximizing Your Wealth through Strategic Financial Management

In the pursuit of financial success and building wealth, tax planning and strategies play a crucial role in maximizing your earnings and achieving your goals. The ability to effectively manage your finances and take advantage of tax-saving opportunities can significantly impact your long-term financial well-being. This subchapter, titled "Tax Planning and Strategies: Maximizing Your Wealth through Strategic Financial Management," aims to provide aspiring entrepreneurs, career professionals, students and young adults, individuals seeking personal growth, financial beginners, small business owners, investors, social educators and mentors, self-help enthusiasts, and individuals seeking a holistic approach, with a comprehensive guide on how to navigate the complex world of taxes and use them to your advantage.

Whether you are starting your own business, advancing your career, or simply looking to establish a solid financial foundation, understanding tax planning and strategies is essential. This subchapter will cover a wide range of topics, including

1. The Importance of Tax Planning: Explore why tax planning is crucial in wealth-building and how it can help you keep more of your hard-earned money.

2. Tax-Saving Strategies for Entrepreneurs: Discover specific tax-saving strategies tailored to entrepreneurs and small business owners, such as deductions, credits, and incentives available to them.

3. Maximizing Personal Tax Benefits: Learn how to optimize personal tax benefits, such as retirement contributions, education expenses, and homeownership deductions.

4. Investment Strategies for Tax Efficiency: Explore investment strategies that can help minimize your tax liabilities while maximizing your returns, such as tax-efficient investing and capital gains management.

5. Tax Planning for Different Life Stages: Understand how your tax planning needs may change as you progress through different life stages, from starting a family to planning for retirement.

6. Working with Tax Professionals: Gain insights into the benefits of working with tax professionals, their role in tax planning and compliance, and how to choose the right professional for your needs.

By implementing effective tax planning and strategies, you can reduce your tax burden, increase your savings, and ultimately accelerate your path to financial success. This subchapter will provide you with the knowledge and tools necessary to make informed decisions, optimize your tax situation, and maximize your wealth through strategic financial management.

Remember, becoming rich is not about doing one magic thing; it's about taking consistent and strategic steps towards financial success. Tax planning and strategies are just one piece of the puzzle, but an essential one that can significantly impact your overall financial well-being. So, join us on this journey of wealth-building and personal growth as we explore the world of tax planning and strategies, empowering you to achieve the financial success you desire.

By implementing effective tax planning and strategies, you can reduce your tax burden, increase your savings, and ultimately accelerate your path to financial success. This subchapter will provide you with the knowledge and tools necessary to make informed decisions, optimize your tax situation, and maximize your wealth through strategic financial management.

Remember, becoming rich is not about doing one magic thing; it's about taking consistent and strategic steps towards financial success. Tax planning and strategies are just one piece of the puzzle, but an essential one that can significantly impact your overall financial well-being. So, join us on this journey of wealth-building and personal growth as we explore the world of tax planning and strategies, empowering you to achieve the financial success you desire.

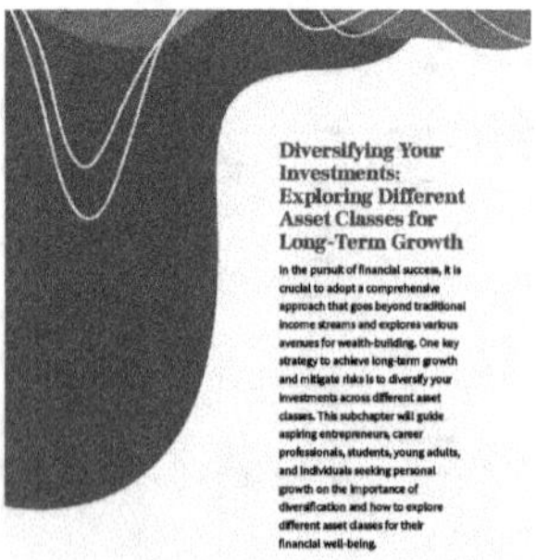

Diversifying Your Investments: Exploring Different Asset Classes for Long-Term Growth

In the pursuit of financial success, it is crucial to adopt a comprehensive approach that goes beyond traditional income streams and explores various avenues for wealth-building. One key strategy to achieve long-term growth and mitigate risks is to diversify your investments across different asset classes. This subchapter will guide aspiring entrepreneurs, career professionals, students, young adults, and individuals seeking personal growth on the importance of diversification and how to explore different asset classes for their financial well-being.

When it comes to investing, many people mistakenly believe that putting all their eggs in one basket is the key to becoming rich. However, this narrow mindset can be detrimental to your long-term financial goals. Diversification is the practice of spreading investments across different asset classes, such as stocks, bonds, real estate, commodities, and alternative investments like cryptocurrencies or peer-to-peer lending platforms. By diversifying your portfolio, you can reduce the potential impact of market volatility and protect yourself against significant losses.

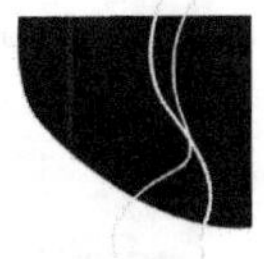

This subchapter will delve into the benefits and challenges of investing in different asset classes. It will explore the characteristics of each asset class, their risk profiles, and potential returns. Readers will gain a deeper understanding of the various investment options available to them and how to tailor their portfolio to their specific financial goals and risk tolerance.

Moreover, this subchapter will provide practical guidance on how to get started with diversifying investments. It will educate readers on the importance of asset allocation, portfolio rebalancing, and staying informed about market trends. Additionally, it will highlight the significance of conducting thorough research, seeking professional advice, and continuously evaluating and adjusting investment strategies.

Whether you are an aspiring entrepreneur looking to grow your wealth, a career professional aiming to enhance your financial well-being, or a student eager to establish a solid financial foundation, this subchapter will equip you with the knowledge and tools necessary to explore different asset classes for long-term growth. By diversifying your investments, you can not only achieve financial success but also gain a sense of security and peace of mind, knowing that your wealth is protected against unforeseen circumstances.

In conclusion, this subchapter serves as an essential guide for individuals from various backgrounds and niches who are seeking to enhance their financial well-being, personal growth, and overall prosperity. It offers valuable insights and practical advice on diversifying investments across different asset classes, empowering readers to make informed choices that align with their goals and aspirations. By adopting a holistic approach to wealth-building and personal development, readers can unlock their full potential and create a future of abundance and fulfillment.

Risk Management: Mitigating Financial Risks and Protecting Your Investments

In the journey towards financial success, understanding and effectively managing risks is crucial. This subchapter delves into the realm of risk management, offering valuable insights and strategies to mitigate financial risks and protect your investments. Whether you are an aspiring entrepreneur, a career professional, a student, or anyone seeking personal growth and financial empowerment, this chapter will equip you with the necessary tools to navigate the uncertain terrain of wealth-building.

For aspiring entrepreneurs, starting a business can be a risky endeavor. This subchapter will guide you through the process of identifying potential risks, assessing their impact on your venture, and implementing risk management strategies to safeguard your investments. From understanding market volatility to managing cash flow and protecting intellectual property, you will learn how to reduce uncertainties and increase the likelihood of success.

Career professionals looking to enhance their financial well-being will gain valuable insights on managing financial risks. Whether it's making informed investment decisions, protecting assets, or planning for retirement, this subchapter will provide you with the knowledge and tools to make sound financial choices, thereby advancing your career and securing your financial future.

If you are a student or a young adult, establishing a solid financial foundation is essential. This subchapter offers guidance on building good financial habits, understanding the principles of wealth-building, and protecting your investments from potential risks. By starting early and making informed decisions, you can set yourself on a path towards long-term financial success.

For those seeking personal growth, this subchapter connects the principles of risk management with self-improvement and mindset enhancement. By understanding and managing financial risks, you can develop a resilient and growth-oriented mindset that transcends monetary success, leading to a more holistic and fulfilling life.

Financial beginners will find this subchapter to be a comprehensive guide, providing step-by-step instructions on identifying and mitigating financial risks. By gaining a solid understanding of risk management principles, you will be empowered to make informed choices, chart your financial journey, and maximize your wealth-building potential.

Small business owners and investors will also benefit from this subchapter, as it offers insights into risk management strategies tailored to their specific needs. From diversifying investment portfolios to implementing contingency plans for business growth, you will learn how to protect and maximize your financial potential.

Social educators and mentors can utilize the insights from this subchapter to guide others towards financial empowerment. By understanding risk management principles and teaching them to others, you can empower individuals to make informed financial decisions, thereby fostering a more financially secure and prosperous society.

For self-help enthusiasts, this subchapter integrates the principles of personal development with financial success. By embracing risk management strategies, you can align your mindset, beliefs, and actions with your financial goals and aspirations, creating a pathway to holistic abundance and fulfillment.

Ultimately, this subchapter offers a multifaceted approach to risk management, making it relevant to a diverse range of readers. By mastering the art of mitigating financial risks and protecting your investments, you can pave the way towards financial success, personal growth, and a more prosperous future.

Legacy Building: Leaving a Lasting Impact and Creating Generational Wealth

In this subchapter, we delve into the concept of legacy building and how it is instrumental in creating generational wealth. We explore the idea that becoming rich is not solely about accumulating financial assets, but also about leaving a lasting impact on the world and creating a sustainable foundation for future generations.

For aspiring entrepreneurs, legacy building is an essential component of long-term success. It involves building a business that goes beyond immediate financial gain and focuses on creating a lasting impact. By aligning their ventures with their values and passions, aspiring entrepreneurs can build a legacy that resonates with their purpose and ensures the longevity of their success.

Career professionals looking to enhance their financial well-being can also benefit from the principles of legacy building. By leveraging their skills, expertise, and connections, they can create opportunities for themselves and others, leaving a lasting impact on their industries. This subchapter offers guidance on how to identify and cultivate their unique strengths to create a legacy that extends beyond their current roles.

Students and young adults seeking a solid financial foundation will learn the importance of starting early and building habits that lead to long-term wealth. By adopting a mindset of legacy building, they can make informed financial decisions that set them on a path towards creating generational wealth. This subchapter provides practical strategies for young people to build assets, invest wisely, and leave a lasting impact on their communities.

For those new to the world of personal finance and wealth-building, this subchapter serves as a comprehensive guide to get started. It covers the fundamental principles of legacy building, including the power of compound interest, strategic investments, and the importance of giving back. By understanding these principles, financial beginners can lay a strong foundation for their wealth-building journey.

Small business owners and investors will discover how legacy building can maximize their financial potential. By focusing on creating sustainable and scalable enterprises, they can build wealth that extends far beyond their own lifetimes. This subchapter provides insights on how to align business strategies with long-term goals and create a legacy that leaves an indelible mark on the world.

Furthermore, this subchapter highlights the importance of a holistic approach to wealth-building. It emphasizes that becoming rich is not just about financial success but also about personal growth, interconnected prosperity, and higher levels of consciousness. By adopting a mindset of abundance and practicing self-improvement, individuals can create a legacy that encompasses all aspects of their lives.

In conclusion, legacy building is a crucial aspect of achieving financial success and personal fulfilment. This subchapter provides a comprehensive guide for individuals from various backgrounds, including aspiring entrepreneurs, career professionals, students, and financial beginners. By understanding the principles of legacy building and aligning their actions with their long-term goals, readers can create a lasting impact, build generational wealth, and ultimately achieve their desired level of financial success.

06

Chapter 6: Creating
a Balanced and
Fulfilling Life

Work-Life Balance: Prioritizing Health, Relationships, and Personal Well-being

In the fast-paced world of entrepreneurship and career advancement, it is easy to get caught up in the pursuit of financial success and overlook other essential aspects of life. However, true wealth and fulfillment extend beyond monetary achievements. In this subchapter, we explore the importance of work-life balance and how prioritizing health, relationships, and personal well-being can contribute to your overall success.

This subchapter offers practical tips and strategies for maintaining physical and mental health, fostering meaningful relationships, and creating boundaries between work and personal life.

For aspiring entrepreneurs, finding a balance between work and personal life is crucial. It is easy to become consumed by the demands of starting and growing a business, but neglecting your health and relationships can have long-term consequences. By prioritizing your well-being, you can maintain the energy, focus, and resilience needed to navigate the challenges of entrepreneurship.

This subchapter offers practical tips and strategies for maintaining physical and mental health, fostering meaningful relationships, and creating boundaries between work and personal life.

Career professionals looking to enhance their financial well-being can also benefit from prioritizing work-life balance. Often, the pursuit of promotions and financial success can lead to burnout and a lack of fulfillment. This subchapter provides guidance on how to set boundaries, manage stress, and find fulfillment in both career and personal life.

For students and young adults, establishing a solid financial foundation is essential. However, it is equally important to prioritize personal growth and well-being from an early age. This subchapter offers insights on how to balance academic and career aspirations with self-care and personal development, setting the stage for a successful and fulfilling future.

Financial beginners will find this subchapter invaluable as it offers a comprehensive guide to getting started on their wealth-building journey. It emphasizes the importance of a holistic approach that encompasses not only financial success but also personal growth, relationships, and health. By prioritizing these areas, individuals can build a strong foundation for long-term financial empowerment.

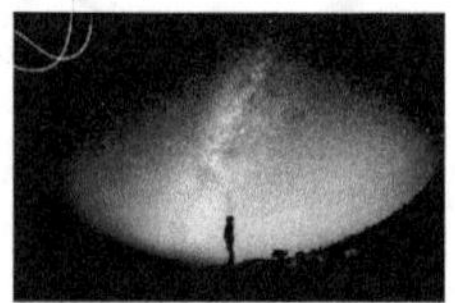

For students and young adults, establishing a solid financial foundation is essential. However, it is equally important to prioritize personal growth and well-being from an early age. This subchapter offers insights on how to balance academic and career aspirations with self-care and personal development, setting the stage for a successful and fulfilling future.

Financial beginners will find this subchapter invaluable as it offers a comprehensive guide to getting started on their wealth-building journey. It emphasizes the importance of a holistic approach that encompasses not only financial success but also personal growth, relationships, and health. By prioritizing these areas, individuals can build a strong foundation for long-term financial empowerment.

Small business owners and investors will also find guidance on work-life balance in this subchapter. It explores strategies for managing the demands of entrepreneurship or investment while maintaining personal well-being and relationships. By adopting a balanced approach, entrepreneurs can maximize their potential for financial success while enjoying a fulfilling personal life.

Overall, this subchapter on work-life balance recognizes that true wealth and success go beyond financial achievements. It provides insights and strategies that can be tailored to individual goals and aspirations, helping readers achieve financial well-being while nurturing their health, relationships, and personal growth. By prioritizing these areas, individuals can create a holistic and fulfilling life that encompasses not only financial success but also personal fulfillment and happiness.

Mindfulness and Stress Management: Cultivating Inner Peace and Resilience

In today's fast-paced and demanding world, stress has become a common companion for many individuals. Entrepreneurs, career professionals, students, and even small business owners often find themselves overwhelmed with the pressures and challenges they face on a daily basis. The need for effective stress management techniques and strategies has never been greater.

This subchapter titled "Mindfulness and Stress Management: Cultivating Inner Peace and Resilience" delves into the power of mindfulness in navigating the turbulent waters of entrepreneurship and financial success. It explores how cultivating inner peace and resilience can not only enhance your overall well-being but also contribute to your financial growth and prosperity.

Mindfulness, the practice of being fully present in the moment, has been proven to reduce stress, improve focus, and enhance decision-making abilities. By incorporating mindfulness into your daily routine, you can develop a greater sense of calm, clarity, and emotional stability, which are essential qualities for success in any venture.

This subchapter offers practical techniques and exercises to help you incorporate mindfulness into your life. From simple breathing exercises to guided meditations, you will discover a range of tools to help you cultivate inner peace and resilience. By practicing mindfulness, you will learn to manage stress more effectively, make better financial decisions, and maintain a positive mindset even in challenging situations.

Furthermore, this subchapter also explores the concept of resilience and its importance in navigating the ups and downs of entrepreneurship and financial endeavors. Resilience is the ability to bounce back from setbacks and adapt to change. By developing resilience, you will be better equipped to handle the inevitable challenges and obstacles that come with the pursuit of financial success.

By reading this subchapter, aspiring entrepreneurs, career professionals, students, and individuals seeking personal growth will gain valuable insights and strategies for managing stress, cultivating inner peace, and developing resilience. These skills are not only essential for achieving financial success but also for leading a balanced and fulfilling life.

In conclusion, "Mindfulness and Stress Management: Cultivating Inner Peace and Resilience" is a subchapter that offers practical tools and techniques for individuals in various niches to enhance their financial well-being and personal growth. By incorporating mindfulness and developing resilience, readers will be better equipped to navigate the challenges of entrepreneurship, make informed financial decisions, and achieve a higher level of consciousness and interconnected prosperity.

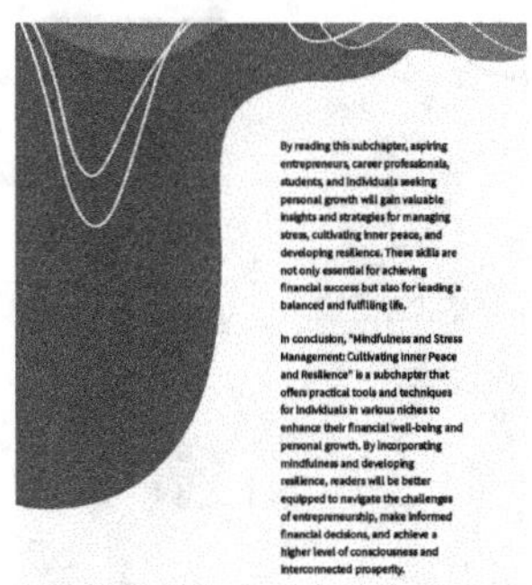

By reading this subchapter, aspiring entrepreneurs, career professionals, students, and individuals seeking personal growth will gain valuable insights and strategies for managing stress, cultivating inner peace, and developing resilience. These skills are not only essential for achieving financial success but also for leading a balanced and fulfilling life.

In conclusion, "Mindfulness and Stress Management: Cultivating Inner Peace and Resilience" is a subchapter that offers practical tools and techniques for individuals in various niches to enhance their financial well-being and personal growth. By incorporating mindfulness and developing resilience, readers will be better equipped to navigate the challenges of entrepreneurship, make informed financial decisions, and achieve a higher level of consciousness and interconnected prosperity.

Giving Back: Embracing Philanthropy and Making a Positive Social Impact

In the pursuit of financial success, it is crucial to not only focus on accumulating wealth but also on giving back and making a positive social impact. Philanthropy plays a significant role in creating a more equitable and prosperous society, and it is a fundamental aspect of wealth-building that aspiring entrepreneurs, career professionals, students, and individuals seeking personal growth should embrace.

Philanthropy goes beyond financial donations. It involves actively engaging in initiatives and causes that align with your values and have a meaningful impact on the community. By giving back, you not only contribute to the greater good but also create a sense of purpose and fulfillment in your own life.

One way to engage in philanthropy is by supporting local nonprofits and charitable organizations that address social issues you are passionate about. Whether it is education, healthcare, poverty alleviation, or environmental conservation, there are numerous causes that can benefit from your time, expertise, and resources. By volunteering or serving on boards, you can make a direct impact and be part of positive change.

Another way to embrace philanthropy is by incorporating social responsibility into your business ventures. As an aspiring entrepreneur or small business owner, you have the power to create positive change through your products, services, and practices. By adopting sustainable and ethical business practices, supporting local suppliers, and giving back a portion of your profits to charitable causes, you can build a business that not only generates wealth but also contributes to the betterment of society.

Furthermore, philanthropy should not be seen as a one-time act but as an ongoing commitment. As your financial success grows, so should your dedication to making a positive social impact. Consider setting aside a portion of your income or profits specifically for philanthropic endeavors, creating a sustainable and long-term approach to giving back.

In conclusion, embracing philanthropy and making a positive social impact should be an integral part of your wealth-building journey. By giving back, you not only contribute to the well-being of others but also enhance your own personal growth and fulfillment. Aspiring entrepreneurs, career professionals, students, and individuals seeking personal growth should recognize the importance of philanthropy and actively engage in initiatives that create a more equitable and prosperous society. By incorporating social responsibility into your business ventures and continuously dedicating resources to philanthropy, you can achieve financial success while making a meaningful difference in the world.

Furthermore, philanthropy should not be seen as a one-time act but as an ongoing commitment. As your financial success grows, so should your dedication to making a positive social impact. Consider setting aside a portion of your income or profits specifically for philanthropic endeavors, creating a sustainable and long-term approach to giving back.

In conclusion, embracing philanthropy and making a positive social impact should be an integral part of your wealth-building journey. By giving back, you not only contribute to the well-being of others but also enhance your own personal growth and fulfillment. Aspiring entrepreneurs, career professionals, students, and individuals seeking personal growth should recognize the importance of philanthropy and actively engage in initiatives that create a more equitable and prosperous society. By incorporating social responsibility into your business ventures and continuously dedicating resources to philanthropy, you can achieve financial success while making a meaningful difference in the world.

Lifelong Learning and Personal Development: Continuously Growing as an Individual

In the journey towards financial success, one key aspect that is often overlooked is the importance of lifelong learning and personal development. It is not enough to simply acquire wealth; true prosperity comes from continuously growing as an individual. This subchapter explores the significance of ongoing education and self-improvement in achieving financial goals and personal fulfillment.

For aspiring entrepreneurs, the path to success is paved with knowledge. Starting your own business or venture requires a strong foundation of skills and expertise. By embracing lifelong learning, you can acquire the necessary knowledge and develop the mindset needed to navigate the challenges and seize opportunities that come your way.

Career professionals looking to advance their financial well-being can benefit greatly from personal development. By continuously honing your skills, expanding your knowledge, and staying abreast of industry trends, you position yourself for better career prospects and higher earning potential. Lifelong learning also empowers you to make informed financial decisions that can lead to long-term financial security.

For students and young adults, establishing a solid financial foundation is paramount. By embracing the principles of wealth-building from an early age, you can set yourself up for a lifetime of financial success. Lifelong learning and personal development provide the tools and mindset needed to make smart financial choices, build wealth, and achieve financial independence.

Personal growth and self-improvement are not limited to financial gain; they are integral to overall well-being and fulfilment. Individuals seeking personal growth can benefit from continuous learning and development, as it enhances mindset, resilience, and adaptability. By investing in your personal growth, you become better equipped to navigate life's challenges, achieve greater financial success, and find true happiness and fulfilment.

No matter where you are on your financial journey, whether you are a financial beginner, a small business owner, an investor, a social educator, or simply someone seeking a holistic approach to wealth and personal growth, this book offers a comprehensive guide. It emphasizes the importance of lifelong learning and personal development in achieving financial success and provides practical insights and strategies tailored to your unique goals and aspirations.

In conclusion, the path to financial success and personal growth is not a one-time event, but a lifelong journey. By embracing continuous learning and personal development, you can continuously grow as an individual, enhance your financial well-being, and achieve greater levels of success, prosperity, and fulfilment.

Achieving Interconnected Prosperity: Aligning Your Financial Success with Higher Purposes

In this subchapter, we explore the concept of interconnected prosperity and how aligning your financial success with higher purposes can lead to a more fulfilling and meaningful life. Whether you are an aspiring entrepreneur, a career professional, a student, or someone seeking personal growth, this chapter offers valuable insights and guidance on how to achieve financial success while staying true to your higher values and purpose.

The traditional notion of financial success often revolves around accumulating wealth and material possessions. While these may bring temporary happiness, true fulfillment comes from aligning our financial endeavors with our higher purposes and values. In this subchapter, we delve into the importance of defining your higher purpose and how it can serve as a driving force behind your financial success.

We explore the concept of interconnected prosperity, which goes beyond individual wealth accumulation and encompasses the well-being and prosperity of others and the planet. By adopting a holistic approach to wealth-building, you can create a positive impact on society and contribute to a more sustainable and equitable world.

Throughout this subchapter, we provide practical strategies and actionable steps to help you align your financial success with higher purposes. We discuss the importance of setting clear goals, developing a growth mindset, and cultivating a strong sense of purpose. We also explore the role of conscious decision-making, ethical business practices, and social responsibility in achieving interconnected prosperity.

Additionally, we address the common misconceptions and limiting beliefs that often hinder individuals from pursuing their higher purposes and achieving financial success. By debunking these myths and providing alternative perspectives, we aim to empower readers to overcome obstacles and unlock their full potential.

Whether you are a financial beginner or an experienced entrepreneur, this subchapter offers valuable insights and practical advice to help you achieve interconnected prosperity. By aligning your financial success with higher purposes, you can create a life of abundance, fulfillment, and contribution. Join us on this transformative journey toward financial success and personal growth.

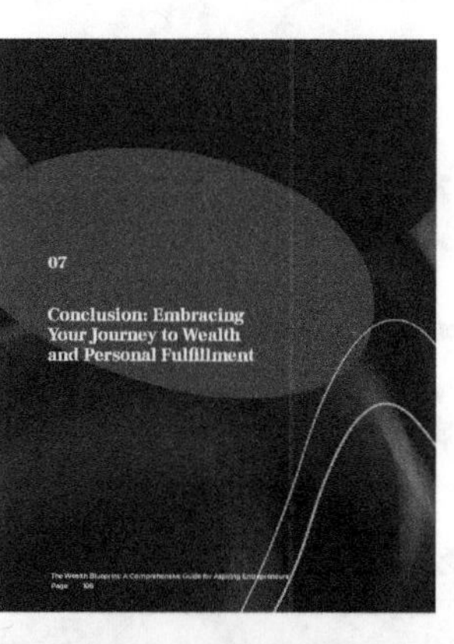

07

Conclusion: Embracing
Your Journey to Wealth
and Personal Fulfillment

In this subchapter, we conclude our comprehensive guide, "The Wealth Blueprint: A Comprehensive Guide for Aspiring Entrepreneurs," with a powerful message to all our readers, regardless of their specific goals and aspirations. We believe that anyone can achieve financial success and personal fulfilment by embracing their unique journey.

Throughout this book, we have covered a wide range of topics, from the fundamentals of personal finance to advanced wealth-building strategies. We have shared insights from successful entrepreneurs, career professionals, investors, and self-help enthusiasts, all coming together to provide you with a holistic approach to achieving your financial goals.

One key message that resonates throughout this book is that becoming rich is not as elusive as it may seem. The path to wealth and personal fulfilment begins with a single step - taking action. By taking that first step, you are already ahead of the majority who remain stuck in their comfort zones, dreaming of financial success without taking any action to make it a reality.

We have emphasized the importance of mindset and personal growth in achieving financial success. By cultivating a growth mindset and continuously seeking self-improvement, you can overcome obstacles, adapt to changes, and unlock your full potential. We have provided tools and strategies to enhance your mindset, such as visualization techniques, gratitude practices, and affirmations, which can be applied to all areas of your life.

Lastly, we have stressed the importance of a holistic approach to wealth and personal fulfilment. True success is not solely measured by financial wealth but also by personal growth, interconnected prosperity, and higher levels of consciousness. By aligning your financial goals with your values, contributing to your community, and cultivating a sense of purpose, you can achieve a more profound and meaningful level of success.

Another crucial aspect we have explored is the power of education and continuous learning. Whether you are a student, a small business owner, or a seasoned professional, investing in your knowledge and skills is essential for long-term success. By staying updated on industry trends, expanding your network, and seeking mentorship, you can gain a competitive edge and open doors to new opportunities.

Lastly, we have stressed the importance of a holistic approach to wealth and personal fulfilment. True success is not solely measured by financial wealth but also by personal growth, interconnected prosperity, and higher levels of consciousness. By aligning your financial goals with your values, contributing to your community, and cultivating a sense of purpose, you can achieve a more profound and meaningful level of success.

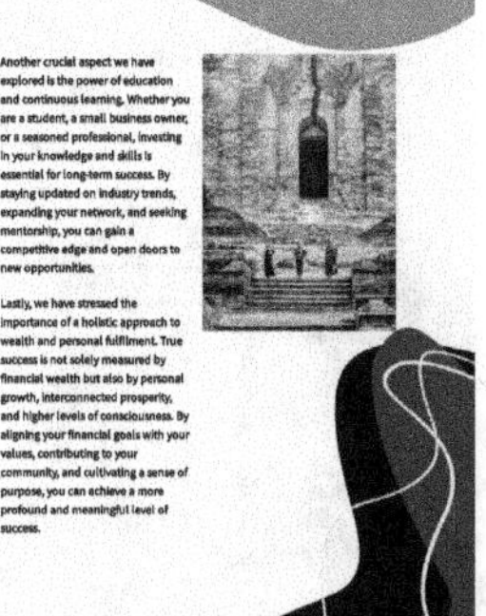

As you conclude this book, we encourage you to reflect on your unique journey and set actionable goals that align with your aspirations. Embrace the challenges, failures, and successes along the way, for they are all part of the path to wealth and personal fulfilment.

Remember, becoming rich is not about a single action or quick fix; it is a lifelong journey of continuous growth and development.

We hope that "The Wealth Blueprint" has provided you with the knowledge, inspiration, and guidance to embark on your own journey to financial success and personal fulfilment. Remember, you have the power to create the life you desire. Embrace your journey, take action, and watch as your dreams become a reality.

The Wealth Blueprint: A Comprehensive Guide for Aspiring Entrepreneurs

Inspiration Source: Mukadam Olaitan Alabi Ajetunmobi Mukadam Olaitan Alabi Ajetunmobi, a luminary in personal transformation and financial empowerment, is the wellspring of inspiration behind this journey. With over 25 years dedicated to transformation and 18 years as a seasoned social educator, Alabi is a testament to the boundless potential within us. His life story, spanning four decades, is a narrative of resilience, wisdom, and unwavering dedication. In "The Wealth Blueprint: A Comprehensive Guide for Aspiring Entrepreneurs," Alabi shares a lifetime of insights, igniting the flames of entrepreneurial success and personal growth. This book is your gateway to unlocking the secrets of financial prosperity and self-improvement. Step into a world where transformation and prosperity are not dreams but living realities. Your journey to entrepreneurial success begins here, guided by Mukadam Olaitan Alabi Ajetunmobi.